David McGuffin

Gary D. McGuffin

GREAT LAKES JOURNEY

OTHER BOOKS BY GARY AND JOANIE McGUFFIN

In the Footsteps of Grey Owl: Journey into the Ancient Forest (2002)

Paddle Your Own Canoe: An Illustrated Guide to the Art of Canoeing (1999)

Superior: Journeys on an Inland Sea (1995)

Where Rivers Run: A 6,000 Mile Exploration of Canada by Canoe (1988)

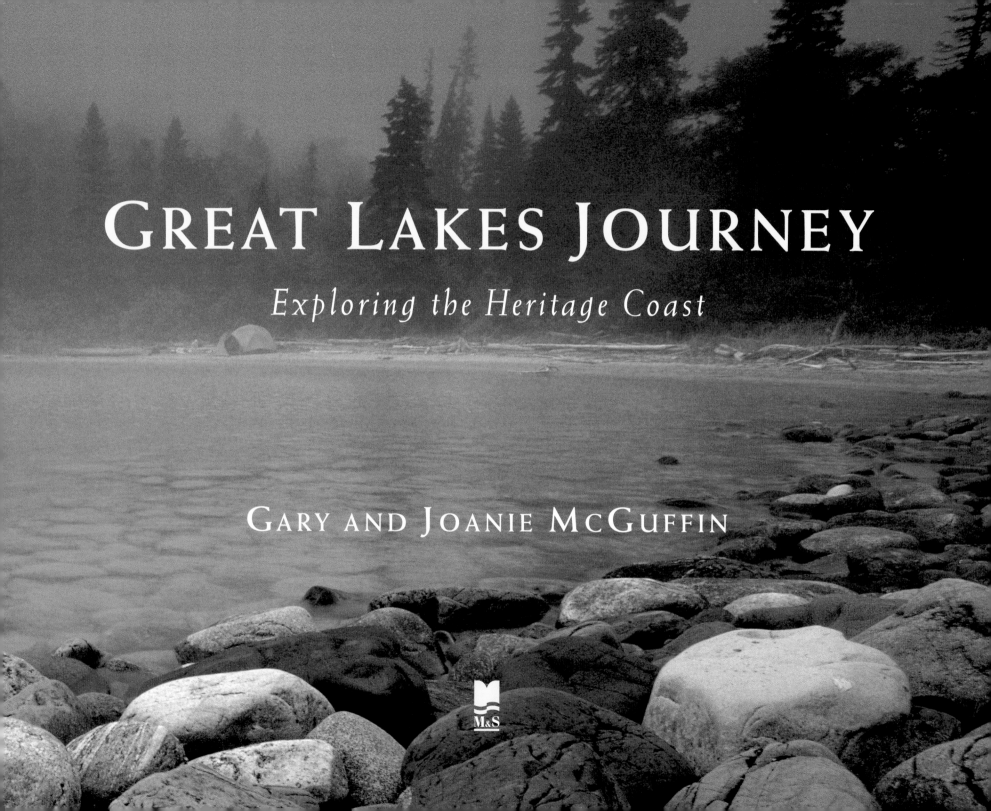

GREAT LAKES JOURNEY

Exploring the Heritage Coast

GARY AND JOANIE McGUFFIN

M&S

National Library of Canada Cataloguing in Publication

McGuffin, Gary
        Great Lakes journey : exploring the Heritage Coast / Gary and Joanie McGuffin.

ISBN 0-7710-5539-0

1. Superior, Lake — Description and travel. 2. North Channel (Huron, Lake, Mich. and Ont.) — Description and travel.
3. Georgian Bay (Ont.) — Description and travel. 4. McGuffin, Gary — Journeys — Great Lakes Region.
5. McGuffin, Joanie — Journeys — Great Lakes Region. I. McGuffin, Joanie II. Title.

FC3095.G724M34 2003   917.1304'4   C2003-903510-7

We acknowledge the financial support of the Government of Canada through the Book Publishing Industry Development Program and that of the Government of Ontario through the Ontario Media Development Corporation's Ontario Book Initiative. We further acknowledge the support of the Canada Council for the Arts and the Ontario Arts Council for our publishing program.

Book design by K.T. Njo
Photographs by Gary McGuffin
Map by Visutronx and Joanie McGuffin

Half-title page: Crossing Thunder Bay to the Sleeping Giant
Title page image: Bottle Cove
Image on pages 8-9: Channel Island and Ogilvy Point north of the Pic River
Image on pages 44-45: Batchawana Bay

Typeset in Bembo by M&S, Toronto
Printed and bound in Hong Kong, China

McClelland & Stewart Ltd.
The Canadian Publishers
481 University Avenue
Toronto, Ontario
M5G 2E9
www.mcclelland.com

1   2   3   4   5   07   06   05   04   03

To all those who care about this place

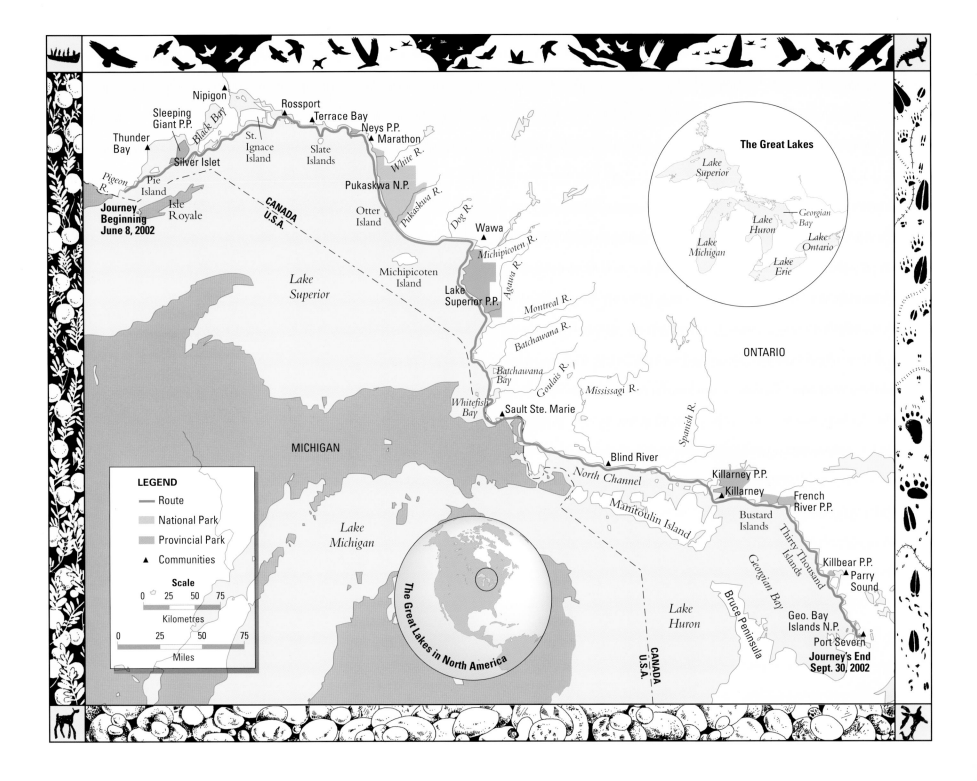

Nipigon

Rossport

Terrace Bay

Sleeping
Giant P.P.

Black Bay

Neys P.P.

Thunder
Bay

St.
Ignace
Island

Marathon

Slate
Islands

Silver Islet

White R.

Pigeon
R.

Pie
Island

Pukaskwa N.P.

Isle
Royale

Pukaskwa R.

**Journey
Beginning
June 8, 2002**

CANADA
U.S.A.

Otter
Island

Dog R.

Wawa

Michipicoten
Island

Michipicoten R.

Agawa R.

Lake
Superior

Lake
Superior P.P.

Montreal R.

Batchawana R.

ONTARIO

Batchawana
Bay

Goulais R.

Mississagi R.

Spanish R.

Whitefish
Bay

Sault Ste. Marie

MICHIGAN

Blind River

North Channel

Killarney P.P.

Killarney

French
River P.P.

Manitoulin Island

Bustard
Islands

The Great Lakes

Lake
Superior

Georgian
Bay

Lake
Huron

Lake
Michigan

Lake
Ontario

Lake
Erie

LEGEND

━━━ Route

National Park

Provincial Park

▲ Communities

Scale

0   25   50   75
Kilometres

0   25   50   75
Miles

Lake
Michigan

The Great Lakes in North America

Georgian Bay

Thirty Thousand Islands

Killbear P.P.

Parry
Sound

Bruce Peninsula

Lake
Huron

Geo. Bay
Islands N.P.

Port Severn

**Journey's End
Sept. 30, 2002**

CANADA
U.S.A.

Contents

THE JOURNEY IN WORDS

Our 6-metre (21-foot)-long Great Lakes canoe was designed and built specifically for the journey, being most efficient to paddle when fully loaded.

PLANNING THE VOYAGE

I remember the morning we met Peter. It was early May 1995, and we arose to the soft sloshing of water against sand, a sound we had not heard for four months. While we were sleeping, an offshore breeze had pushed persistently at the ice sheet covering Batchawana Bay and sent it drifting out into the big lake.

At the time we were living on the east shore of Lake Superior. Every morning it was our ritual to walk along Harmony Beach to the mouth of the Harmony River to say good morning to the day. As we were making our way back, we noticed a school bus and a Ministry of Natural Resources truck turning in from Highway 17. They followed the curve of the beach road to the pull-in opposite our home. Teenagers filed off the bus. When we reached them, they were clustered around a patch of dune grass. Kalija, our Alaskan Malamute, nosed up behind the sturdy man in the centre of the activity. Surprised, he turned towards us with a big grin. He was bearded, red-haired, and dressed in typical northern garb: a check wool shirt, jeans, and work boots. "Hi, I'm Peter Burtch," he announced.

As we soon learned, this high-school Adopt-a-Beach program was one of many projects that Peter had been involved in as a specialist in shoreline ecosystems. More than twenty years ago, he became particularly interested in Whitefish, Goulais,

and Batchawana bays and their underlying Jacobsville sandstone. This part of the shoreline is unique to Lake Superior. Owing to their shallow nature, the bays are relatively warm, and historically have been a tremendous nursery ground for spawning fish and a vast staging area for waterfowl. For centuries, this was of prime importance to the aboriginal people who had arrived from near and far to take advantage of the abundant plant and animal life.

Today, the popularity of the bays hasn't diminished, but it is humans that dominate. Twenty years ago, it was a common practice for shoreline owners to remove rocks, alter shoreline, drain wetlands, damage cobble beaches, dig ditches, and build docks wherever they pleased. This was having a detrimental effect on the natural barrier to shoreline erosion and was destroying important shoreline fish habitat. At that time, the Ministry of Natural Resources was not doing anything to protect the shoreline, so Peter took the initiative and, in 1990, drew up the Sault Ste. Marie District Shoreline Management Plan, which blended shoreline engineering with environmental protection for the coast, and pushed to get these guidelines adopted. This was a first for the Ministry of Natural Resources. Over the next few years, Peter participated on provincial teams to develop the regulations that, if enforced and combined with education, would mean protection for the coast.

In the summer of 1997, Canada was seven years into World Wildlife Fund Canada's Endangered Spaces Program; Ontario, along with most of the provinces, was failing miserably in an effort to protect the country's diversity of ecosystems. Our own Ontario government was earning a D. Partly in response to this, a massive land-use planning process called Lands for Life had been launched by the province, the outcome of which would affect the future of Ontario's remaining wilderness. World Wildlife Fund Canada, the Wildlands League, and the Federation of Ontario Naturalists had mobilized, under the umbrella name of the Partnership for Public Lands, to involve members of the public in the Lands for Life process and increase awareness of the importance of preserving Ontario's ecological diversity. That same summer, Gary and I, along with Kalija, canoed 1,900 kilometres (1,200 miles) along a route that linked some of this continent's finest remaining ancient forest landscapes. The purpose of our journey was to garner public support for protection of these forests, and we would transmit our story while paddling the route. We carried a satellite phone, laptop computer, digital camera, and solar panels, which enabled us to write weekly newspaper stories, give weekly radio interviews, and keep a Web site.

While the three Lands for Life committees representing three planning areas canvassed the province gathering public input, Peter Burtch noticed a major omission in the discussions and debate. One of the Earth's most unique landscapes, the Great Lakes shoreline, was not being recognized to its potential, nor was there any scenario being presented that linked the vast province of Ontario together. A grand vision was needed.

In March 1998, Peter wrote a discussion paper, "Supporting a Great Lakes Shoreline Recognition," which proposed that the Great Lakes coast be acknowledged as an important Ontario asset. The purpose of this endeavour was to protect the unique natural, cultural, and ecological values of the shoreline from the Pigeon River on Lake Superior to the Severn River on Georgian Bay. Peter suggested that increasing public knowledge and appreciation, and directing our human use of the Great Lakes in an ecological way, would be the key to maintaining a healthy shoreline ecosystem for many generations to come. He and his wife, Maureen, entitled this vision "Great Lakes Heritage Coast."

Peter picked up the phone and gave us a call. "What do you think of this idea?" he asked. Gary responded without hesitation: "Peter, if the government adopts this, we'll paddle it in celebration of its protection." By the time our daughter, Sila, was born in the summer of 1999, the Ontario government had announced a proposal to create 378 new parks and protected places, nine of which would receive special status as "signature sites." The Great Lakes Heritage Coast was one of these.

When Sila was six months old, the Ontario government appointed us as official Champions of the Coast under the Great Lakes Heritage Coast program. We accepted the title, and began planning our summer's voyage to explore the Heritage Coast by canoe. The successful broadcasting of our 1997 Ancient Forest journey had laid the foundation for our ability – through the media and the Internet – to help raise public awareness. We felt there was nothing like a journey to capture people's imagination, and the fact that this time we would be travelling with our child would add an extra level of interest.

◄○►

In December 2001, we arrived in Parry Sound at Pam Wedd's Bearwood Canoes workshop to pick up the cedar we needed to build our special Great Lakes canoe. Gary and our friend and boat-builder, Skipper Izon, had worked out a design on paper. We knew Skipper would build us an efficient hull, perfectly suited to the "big water" conditions we would face on the Great Lakes. Our canoe had to be large enough to safely transport 360 kilograms (800 pounds): our family, our communications and camera equipment, our camping supplies, and up to two weeks' worth of food at a time. Also, while loaded, she had to have plenty of freeboard, meaning her gunwales would be 28 centimetres (11 inches) above the surface to avoid swamping. But she also had to be light and fast enough to paddle comfortably on a long voyage. The flare designed into her bow, lovingly dubbed "spray wings," would give it added buoyancy without sacrificing speed. Amidst drifting snow, we loaded the pile of cedar planks on top of Skipper's truck, and he headed south to his workshop in Grand Bend, where months of work lay ahead to actually construct the canoe.

We first laid eyes on our glowing cedar-wood canoe the following spring, when Skipper delivered her to our home on Lake Superior. Our maiden voyage on nearby Robertson Lake was a memorable afternoon. First, Skipper presented Sila with a special paddle sized to fit her height and grip. I had painted her namesake kestrel on the blade. With amazement, we watched her take the paddle and, without prompting, run to the canoe, where she clambered over the edge onto the bow seat and acted

Sometimes Sila and I would go on short explorations along the shore. Using a paddle sized just for her meant that her constant experimentation with the blade's action on the water was giving her the true feel of paddling a canoe.

out the motion of paddling. She had not been in a canoe nor held a paddle since the previous summer, when she was two. There was no one on the lake as we circled, quietly enjoying the birdsong of warblers and a winter wren, then paddled to the lake's far end, where we stopped for lunch. Later, we hoisted the spinnaker, which promptly filled with a tailwind, and we sailed back to the landing.

Getting ready for the day's adventures on the water

THE JOURNEY

Pigeon Bay, Lake Superior, July 8, 2002

A group of folks in authentic voyageur costumes from Old Fort William, friends, and park staff bid us farewell from Pigeon River Provincial Park. They had gathered at the shore, watching with some amazement as we loaded the canoe with pack after pack. Finally, I placed Sila in the bow and took my place on the bow seat. Kalija jumped in behind me, and Gary positioned himself in the stern. To the playing of bagpipes and a musket salute, we pushed off towards the open lake.

We were happy to be under way. We had spent several very feverish, sleepless weeks finding funding, packing packs, acquiring and learning new technology, and distributing supply parcels along the route. The solar panels were laid out on top of the packs, charging the twelve-volt battery, which would power the satellite phone, digital camera, and laptop computer we would use to post daily submissions and photographs on our Web site, write articles for numerous newspapers, and speak weekly with CBC Radio. It would be our way of introducing people to the Heritage Coast. We felt both elation and a great weight of responsibility.

We circled the Boundary Islands, named for their close proximity to the Minnesota-Ontario border. A silhouetted lineup of double-crested cormorants perched along a ridge watching us warily. More herring and ring-billed gulls fluttered upwards in a swirling dance. We had only a quick glimpse of fuzzy grey chicks before they disappeared into rock fissures like the Ojibwa tricksters, the Maymaygwayshi. Farther up the shore, in Big Trout Bay, we paddled in the cool, blue shadows of fantastic cliffs and red slate formations. Ancient cedar trees spiralled out from geometric rock shapes growing well above the reach of storm waves.

By the time we made camp that first evening on a promontory between Cloud Bay and Victoria Island, a fog had crept in. The string of islands receding to distant Pie Island was covered as gently as children lying beneath a soft white duvet. Then the warm sun's light suddenly faded, disappearing behind the high hills of the Nor'Westers. We sat quietly, cradling our mugs of tea. Kalija stretched out on the flat rocks, grunting contentedly as Sila scratched her behind the ears.

◄◦►

At the beginning of our journey, the weather was warm and gentle. Instead of taking our intended route, following the shoreline around Thunder Bay, we were encouraged by the perfect paddling conditions to explore the outer islands whose eastern shores bear the mark of big storms. On Spar Island, we left the canoe and hiked a well-worn trail to a viewpoint at the island's north end, known locally as the Top of the World. From that tabletop rock, all around us the island dropped 75 metres (250 feet) straight to the water. From these precipitous cliffs, we viewed a speckling of reefs, rocks, and small islets, bearing such intriguing names as Moonshine, Slipper, Swan, and Prefontaine. We had a clear view to Thompson Island, Pie Island, the Nor'Westers, and Mount McKay, in aboriginal tradition the ancient residence of the thunderbirds.

At Turtle Point on the tip of Pie Island, we left the safety of shore and struck out for Thunder Cape at the southern end of the Sleeping Giant, 12 kilometres (7 miles) across open water. We set a stiff pace, never breaking stride. Despite our familiarity with Lake Superior, we were never complacent when it came to the weather, which could change at the snap of a finger. The water beneath us was take-your-breath-away cold. Many times we have watched thick fog creep in from the lake, causing the temperature to drop twenty degrees in minutes, even on the calmest, hottest summer's day.

Sila's space in front of me was small but comfortable. A non-porous foam pad was laid out for both her and Kalija. A soft bag containing warm, dry clothes acted as a pillow or seat. Sila had her own fanny pack in which she stuffed snacks, drinks, and treasures collected en route. As the journey progressed, I would be constantly amazed at the inventiveness of our three-year-old in the canoe's bow.

In an hour and a half, we reached Thunder Cape and could see its bird observatory. It was quiet now, but in May the sky is a magical highway of migrating songbirds, ducks, geese, hawks, and eagles arriving to breed and nest between here and the high Arctic. Thousands of birds have been banded here to track migration routes and patterns.

With strawberries and ice cream tucked into his kayak hatch, Andrew, a friend from Thunder Bay, paddled out from the village of Silver Islet to meet us in Tee Harbour. We camped together, and early the following morning Gary and Andrew packed lunches, water, and photographic gear for their hike to the top of the Sleeping Giant. Shortly after leaving the beach, they reached a meadow still invisible beneath the damp breath of dawn. Then, as the air warmed, the veil of fog lifted to reveal a sea of purple and green. This is a seasonal highlight of Sleeping Giant Provincial Park's lowland marshes – the blooming of the wild irises known as blue flags. These marshes and the deep, moist valleys of the peninsula support many plant species, including some thirty kinds of orchids, two rare in Ontario, and thirty-eight different ferns.

When Gary and Andrew reached the top of the trail, they were standing at the lip of Ontario's highest vertical cliffs, a dizzying 250 metres (800 feet) straight down to Lake Superior. Rare peregrine falcons nest here.

The view is most amazing if you imagine what the landscape looked like thirteen thousand years ago when the Great Lakes Basin was still filled with the last of the Wisconsin glacial ice. Entire watersheds were shaped, and the top of the Sleeping Giant emerged. As this ice slowly melted, a colossal weight was lifted off the land, causing the north shore to rise in a process called isostatic rebound – something that continues to this day. And one sunrise long, long ago, the first human inhabitants walked onto this place. We know so very little about them except they were hunters of caribou and gigantic elk, and they travelled here at the edge of the receding glaciers. Although eleven thousand years seems impossibly long ago, we do have a touchstone with these human inhabitants. Near here at a place called the Cummins Site, we once visited a flint-knapping area, where the Paleo-Indian people converged to make stone tools and spear points.

A late-afternoon wind grew brisk after a brief stopover in Silver Islet east of Tee Harbour. Swells rolling down the protected channel just outside the harbour unnerved us. We returned to shore and, by good fortune, Kalija "introduced" us to some local cottagers, Jim Coslett and his daughter Michele Coslett Goodman.

Silver Islet's silver-mining history began one spring day in the early 1870s when John Morgan exposed a rich vein of silver while working with his pickaxe on a small island 1.6 kilometres (1 mile) offshore.

Jim Coslett, who had spent his childhood summers here, showed us his collection of old mining-town photographs, sharing with us his family's connection to Silver Islet. He pointed out two of the square timber mine houses that still stand today.

For more than a decade, the mine operated as the richest silver mine in the world, but ironically the expense of running it was equivalent to the value that came out in silver. The mine's final demise came when a ship bearing coal to keep the pumps running failed to reach Silver Islet, and the mine flooded. Most families left after its closure, with Jim's being one of the few to remain. Today, many of the summer residents share a common bond: it was their ancestors who mined the silver.

◄◦►

Late one afternoon, two days after leaving Silver Islet, we made camp on an island with a view north to the Black Bay Peninsula and west to The Paps, a pair of comfortably rounded hills. Our wooden canoe was resting on the two canvas-covered pads we had made to protect the hull as it lay on rock. We looked

Nature provides an endless array of toys and games. I soon discovered a beach of driftwood and stones needed only our imagination for a lot of fun.

for easy places to pull our vessel ashore in the same way we imagined travellers in bark canoes had done. Places that are appealing to camp now – sheltered from the wind, with a flat, dry spot to set up the tent and easy access to the water from shore – are usually the places people have been camping at for a very long time. If the fishing, berry-picking, wild game, and waterfowl were also historically abundant, aboriginal people most assuredly had used these areas for centuries, if not millennia. If they stopped on this island and the fishing was good, they might even have stayed here many weeks.

On this little sheltered curve of beach, Sila swam with her doll, Sally, and played with stones and shells. While poking at the bank with a stick, she dislodged a thin, curved shard of pottery. She picked it up for a closer look and then showed us her find. It appeared to be a pot rim impressed with a pattern made with a cord-wrapped stick, perhaps a thousand years old.

Early the next morning, before sunrise, the rumbling of an approaching storm woke Gary and me. To the east, pink lightning stabbed the land beyond Nipigon Strait again and again. The electricity arched, then sprayed outwards, with single bright bolts dancing wildly southward. The most powerful force in nature was putting on a memorable show with not a drop of rain. Somewhere, we knew, the dry, resinous boreal forest had been set ablaze. Fire, though to be feared, is in this forest as essential and natural as wind and water – its heat opens conifer seed cones, burns off harmful parasites, and exposes the mineral soils favoured by many plant species.

Our chosen route down into Black Bay took us past Otter Cove. On Shesheeb Point, Gary set up his tripod for the digital photographs necessary to create a 360-degree panoramic view of the bay for our Web site. These photographs were transferred to the laptop computer and sent by satellite phone back to our Webmaster in Sault Ste. Marie. Later in the day that scene would appear on computer screens around the world.

We drifted in quietly towards a cow moose and her calf wading knee-deep across a shallow bay. The mother stopped to feed on aquatic plants while the calf headed for shore to wait in the shadow of the trees. We could have watched them longer, but a pair of snorting otters alerted the cow, which then signalled to her calf of danger and off they strode into the forest. Later as we circled back towards the open lake, Kalija stiffened, sniffing, ears cocked. Sila stopped singing and stared intently in the same direction as Kalija. Suddenly three otters burst from the forest and hurled themselves one at a time into the air, landing with belly-flops on the water. They snorted and snuffled, investigating us from a distance. Sila laughed heartily for a long time afterwards.

Over the next few days, we paddled across the Nipigon

Channel and along the south shore of St. Ignace Island, past Squaw Bay, Bowman Island, and Paradise Island, through Armour Harbour, across Moffat Strait, and along Simpson Island's south shore. Between Grotto Point and Woodbine Harbour, there is a most impressive example of six-sided columnar basalt. On other trips, we have been able to get out and walk about on this rock honeycomb, but today we were being jostled in the turbulence created by waves rebounding off the rocky shore. Outcroppings of this geologic feature are visible along the coast all the way from Pie Island, but this example rivals the Giant's Causeway on the coast of Northern Ireland.

In McKay Cove, Sila's enthusiasm for a swim to a nearby island was contagious. I put her lifejacket on her, and we all kicked and splashed our way across. We skipped flat stones and then swam back. The day was very hot. Kalija scratched out in a cool, hollow spot beneath the trees while we went searching for agates on the outer beaches. These stones, washed down from volcanic bluffs millions of years ago, have been polished smooth by the tumbling of the lake. The colours are delicate, rich, and organic. The patterns in agates hint at the curving silhouettes of the islands, the layered waves of receding beach lines, or the striped bands of colour on a sunset's horizon.

Later, a blood-red moon floated over Morn Bay like an escaped balloon. We watched, fascinated. The moon mysteriously appeared and disappeared behind what we thought at first was fog. On our 7-kilometre (4-mile) crossing to Battle Island the following day, we had only the faint outline of land and the regular pattern of three flashes from the lighthouse to guide us. Then, strangely, we paddled through a distinct wall separating the gloom from the clear sky, and we could see that the entire north shore from Terrace Bay westwards into Nipigon Bay was filled with smoke. Somewhere, a forest was

Some of the world's finest examples of the six-sided, honeycomb-shaped columnar basalt are found on Lake Superior's north shore.

burning. The lighthouse buildings of Battle Island suddenly jumped out in sharp relief, red-and-white structures against blue water and green trees.

Bert Saasto, the lighthouse keeper, was on his morning walk around the island with his dog, Smokey, when we paddled into the harbour. For more than a decade we have been visiting Bert. He told us that the forest fire was in the Steel River valley north of Terrace Bay, ignited by one of those lightning strikes we had watched several mornings before. The dry, hot winds were fanning the fire and smoke westwards.

We climbed three flights of steps to the top of the light-house, 60 metres (200 feet) above the lake, for a sweeping view of this spectacular island archipelago. These enchanted islands are part of a conservation story for which, at the time of writing, there still has not been a resolution between the provincial and federal governments. It is a goal of the Canadian government to establish twenty-nine protected marine regions across Canada. World Wildlife Fund Canada is focusing efforts on a ten-year campaign to challenge the country to accomplish this goal, just as it did through the 1990s with its Endangered Spaces Program to protect terrestrial ecosystems. For five long years, Parks Canada has been working with the people of Lake Superior's north shore to establish Canada's fourth national marine-conservation area. Now, despite the fact that the project has received an unprecedented level of local support, essential for the success of any conservation initiative, the provincial and federal governments have yet to finalize an agreement. This Lake Superior National Marine Conservation Area, combined with the American waters around Isle Royale National Park, would form the largest protected area of freshwater on the Earth. This federal designation, in concert with the provincial Great Lakes Heritage Coast initiative, would give this area the strongest level of protection – a legacy for the future. However, in the years that this painfully drawn-out process has been taking place, some of the most beautiful, culturally and ecologically rich islands have become privately owned. It is now in the hands of these citizens to leave a legacy for the future by ensuring that the conservation value overrides monetary gain.

In many places, we came ashore on these islands to hike to a viewpoint or to explore a beach. Some distance up from the lake, we arrived at the storm strand marking the line of a lakeshore thousands of years old. Within this wavy line, we found pieces of shipwreck, fishnet floats, and rope. Beyond the line were the broad and ancient rock terraces, some as huge as football fields. The rocks were encrusted with green, black, and grey lichen. The most extraordinary thing about these terraced beaches was the Pukaskwa pits.

Long, long ago, people dug up rocks from the beaches and piled them around the shallow pits they created. The pit we stood near now had raised walls and was big enough that we could imagine a hunter crouching down inside.

Other pits lie level with the beach, but they are deep enough that people could have spent a night inside with an animal skin covering, or perhaps used them to store food. On higher, exposed parts of some beaches, there are shallow depressions. The aboriginal people of today attest that these pits were used for spiritual journeys – vision quests and fasts.

After setting up camp one evening, we rock-hopped near the water's edge. Sila and I climbed to the top of one of the largest arches to be found along the North Shore. We stepped carefully, knowing carelessness leaves the imprint of our footsteps in the slow-growing lichen for generations. On one side of the arch, the moon rose. On the other, the silhouette of a wavering line of ducks in flight passed before the setting sun.

At the village of Rossport, we had left the first of our seven supply parcels with my sister's family, who live on nearby Nicol Island. When their home came into sight, Sila squirmed with excitement. I had to explain that her cousins were away, but we would be meeting them in several more days a little farther east at Neys Provincial Park. The moment we touched shore, she was out of the canoe and hurrying up the path, with Kalija right behind her. At the top of the hill, Sila found her Uncle Tim clad in his big white potter's apron, placing fresh wildflowers in his large vases. His pottery surrounded him in this outdoor shop: large plates, decorated with my sister's stylized drawings of moose, birds, and flowers; mugs and goblets and pots of various sizes, all in colours reminiscent of Superior – deep blues, greens, and earthy browns. By the time Gary and I had portaged everything up to the covered porch, Sila had made a couple of pinch pots with Tim. How much more the discovery of thousand-year-old clay pottery shards in the islands would mean to her now!

Loon cries echoed lonely in the fog as we paddled away from Nicol Island, passing our favourite swimming beaches and the Rossport Campground. We hugged the shore looking for a place we remembered from the previous summer, when all of a sudden, out of the fog, it appeared. Flint Island in Schreiber Channel marks the shoreline location of a Provincial Nature Reserve established to protect one of North America's most significant occurrences of ancient fossils. The water was too rough to pull the canoe up, so Gary timed the rise and fall of the waves and seized the chance to step out with his camera box. I held the canoe a safe distance away from shore. We could all see the concentric circles on the rocks close to the waterline. Some were up to a metre (3 feet) in diameter. Of the two dozen known sites in the world, this example of stromatolites is the best. These fossilized blue-green algae colonies formed in coastal areas, and from them all life was derived. They were the Earth's earliest oxygen-consuming life forms.

The basin in which the Great Lakes lie is complex. The rocks hold the story of the planet's origins. But the glaciers scoured away the evidence of life's evolution. The fossil record of the Great Lakes Heritage Coast leaps directly from the stromatolites to the era of the Ice Age hunter.

We crossed Collingwood Bay from Twin Harbours to Schreiber Point, with Mount Gwynne dead ahead. From Schreiber Point to Worthington Bay, an already-strong tailwind increased, making us wish we had snapped the canoe cover on before leaving that morning. Several times the canoe raced so quickly down the face of a wave that it plunged headlong into the next one. The bow deck was completely awash. We were all thankful to tuck into Worthington Bay.

A low cliff of smooth grey rock rises from the back of this short, steep beach. At the base, there are red ochre paintings of circles, animal shapes, and people. One particular figure has his arms outstretched. His hands and fingers are large. He is dancing and waving, as he appears to jump across the rock. Nearby there is an ochre pit where, long ago, the painter acquired his natural pigment. Once mixed with sturgeon oil or bear grease, this weather-resistant paint bonded his art to Superior's shore.

In the island oasis of Les Petits Écrits, we found bright-purple harebells and blueberries, but not the small paintings after which the place was named. It was here that we held a birthday celebration for Sila. We lit three candles on three chocolate cupcakes that Tim had made for the occasion while we were in Rossport. Sila opened small gifts, including two hand puppets, a package of tiny books, and her very own flashlight.

We passed Terrace Bay some distance offshore. As its name suggests, there are terraces in the sandy, gravelly material. These were marked off by the wave action at changing water levels – a processs that began shortly after the last glacier melted away. Natural iron deposits oozing from the rocks through this area between Terrace and Victoria bays has left a pattern of rusty-coloured stripes along the headlands and around the rocky points. The landscape here is spectacular. Everything is perfect – except for the fact that there is a paper mill in Terrace Bay. We carefully filtered every drop of our water through here. We only had to see the white plume above the town and catch a whiff of the rotten-egg stench to know that all life along the coast is still being compromised, as it has been for fifty years. And the compromise would be unnecessary if there were the political will for change. Totally chlorine-free processes for bleaching paper have been successfully used for two decades now.

The Slate Islands are 13 kilometres (8 miles) offshore across Jackfish Channel. On the map, they form a roughly circular archipelago of more than twenty-five islands. There is a lighthouse on the south shore of Patterson Island dating back to 1902. In the 1930s, the Slate Islands were logged for pulpwood and, as we paddled over McGreevy Harbour's clear waters, we could see an abundance of sunken logs. In the same bay was the site of a logging camp and barge. McColl Island housed the coal docks and a coal yard. There are many inland lakes on the islands, providing habitat for a great variety of birdlife, but it is the woodland caribou for which the islands are now famous. Their trails on the largest island, Patterson, criss-cross the interior in a virtual maze, and the pattern of trails that the caribou use to swim between the islands is very specific. To watch them, just patiently wait in the canoe at dusk near one of these swimming places.

On long shoreline hikes, I would carry the pack basket, which served as a place for found treasures, and for Sila when she got tired.

The geography, topography, and geology around Prairie Cove, Prince Point, and McKellar Harbour in the larger Ashburton Bay are a fantastic part of the coast. In the striations of the bedrock, caused by the movement of ice, there grows a subarctic plant, the insectivorous butterwort. The flat leaves attract insects, which, once stuck on the greasy surface, are dissolved by secretions from the plant.

The fog drifted in again before we reached the Little Pic River, but we knew it was close by the sight of the sediment in the water, which turns the clear blue-green of McKellar Harbour sandy and opaque. The river carves a very straight path for its final 5 kilometres (3 miles) to the lake, following a geological fault. In fact, the name Pic means "muddy river," and it's a very appropriate name for both the Little Pic and the Pic, both of which flow through clay that was deposited at the bottom of a once-huge lake, much larger than present-day Lake Superior.

Beyond the Little Pic, we coasted along the wide white beach at Neys Provincial Park. At the far end of the beach, where the bay curls around to a point, is Prisoner's Cove. Tucked back in from shore, where rows of red pine now grow, was the site of a Second World War prisoner-of-war camp. Sixty years ago, German soldiers were brought to the isolation of the north shore by train. They were offered jobs with the Pigeon River Lumber Company, working for a dollar a day. Many of them enjoyed the landscape so much they returned with their families after the war ended. Gary and I were thinking about this, but Sila had her mind on only one thing, meeting her cousins, Fae and Mirabai, whom we had missed in Rossport, and who were waiting with my sister here at Neys Provincial Park on that beautiful beach. Scrambling from the canoe, Sila dashed towards them. The three girls ran down the beach together chasing the gulls, jumping over logs, rushing into the waves. Later they nibbled on dried apples by the campfire, quiet and reflective, until finally they crawled into their sleeping bags.

The sun was high and warm the next morning when we packed to depart. The girls had one last swim and then they all helped load the canoe, with Sila telling them where to put things. Then, to my amazement, Sila simply hugged her cousins and her aunt, climbed aboard, and waved goodbye. And that, for Sila, was to be the pattern in making departures for the rest of the voyage.

By the time we turned east around Guse Point on the Coldwell Peninsula, the fog had rolled in again. Pic Island, just across Thompson Channel, seemed to float mysteriously. Group of Seven artist Lawren Harris immortalized that island in 1924. In his large painting, he set Pic Island in a pool of white light and heightened its perspective considerably, giving that sense of enchantment the island most certainly portrays.

The isolation of this area has made it a refuge for wildlife. Between Foster Island and the Coldwell Peninsula, there are sandy, shallow channels just deep enough for a canoe to glide over. On the narrow margin between lake and forest, we found hand-sized wolf prints pressed into the wet sand, and we followed them along the shore. On two occasions we saw caribou. One was just leaving the water. It took its time climbing to a knoll, hooves clattering on the rocks. Another caribou was standing on the edge of Foster Island, facing Pic. Waves were awash about its legs, and the wind was in its face. It appeared to be waiting for calmer weather, like us.

Two days later we paddled into Peninsula Harbour where Marathon's pulp-and-paper mill operates. Here pristine nature gives way to the effects of industry. The pall of smoke, that rotten-egg strench, and the effluent that continues to flow into Lake Superior compromises the health of all living things. The toxins are accumulating in humans and wildlife. There is no avoiding the fact that dioxins, a by-product of North America's chlorine papermaking industry, are the most toxic of substances man has ever created. Only eliminating their use will help.

Pukaskwa National Park, August 2

In Hattie Cove at the national park headquarters, we met up with our good friends Ken and Rilla Zak, with their fox terrier, Oscar. Ken and Rilla had arrived from Wisconsin ready to join us on this leg of our journey down the Pukaskwa coast. It was a long-dreamed-of adventure for them. For us, it was an opportunity to share a treasured place and return to many favourite haunts found over the years on other journeys.

Our first day together, we could not get out of Hattie Cove

In Pukaskwa National Park, Joanie, Sila, and Kalija find a trapper's cabin tucked into the forest away from the lake. Speculations about his life became the source for much storytelling in the canoe.

for wind, so we hiked the headland trails between beach coves and found marvellous viewpoints. We watched huge waves tumble in. The colours were steel grey and blue, reminding me of Canada's east coast. At the end of one beach, we climbed up and slid down a natural slide of tiger-striped rock, smooth as polished glass. We do not know of another example like it anywhere on Lake Superior.

Later that day, we met an elder from Pic River First Nation, who showed us a map with the original Ojibwa names along the coast. They rolled off her tongue, soft and guttural. Pukaskwa is *Bukazhaawe*, pronounced Puk-shay-wa, meaning "the cleaning of fish." We learned Hattie Cove is *Bii to bii gong*, meaning "water between two rocks." This beautiful language describes the features of the landscape – landmarks, rivers, lakes, hills, cliffs – as do all aboriginal languages around the world. I call them the languages of the land. If you know the language, then the names of places are almost a map in themselves. Naming landscape features after people is not very useful.

The next day we packed the canoes and pushed off from Hattie Cove. The fog was thickening, and I felt apprehensive for Ken and Rilla. There were swells left over from the previous day, and riding a canoe rising and falling on Lake Superior is a very different sensation than paddling in waves on a small lake.

Pukaskwa National Park encompasses 1,878 square kilometres (725 square miles) of Canadian Shield and boreal forest and some of the grandest shoreline in the world. The colours of the landscape are vivid, and the view of the sunsets just perfect. After an hour, we turned upstream onto the White River to see Chigamiwinigum Falls, meaning "first portage from the lake." The water was instantly warmer and tea-coloured. Overhead, a pair of pigeon hawks dove with repeated high-pitched calls. At the base of the falls, tons of drift and sunken pulp logs were testimony to the extent to which this river was used for log drives in the 1920s. We left our canoes at the base of the falls and hiked to the suspension bridge where the Pukaskwa coastal hiking trail crosses the river. For anyone lacking a head for heights, it is a knee-shaking experience. Between your feet are open slats and a view 30 metres (100 feet) down into the gorge of Chigamiwinigum Falls.

◄○►

In two days, we covered the distance between White River and Oiseau Bay, and then on to Cascade Falls. We were finally blessed with some calm weather, and we were grateful that Ken and Rilla appreciated completely the necessity to travel when the weather was right and stay put when it wasn't.

In Oiseau Bay, we met three Pukaskwa National Park wardens doing the annual count of Pitcher's thistle, a provincially threatened plant species found on the open sand dunes and low beach ridges of the Great Lakes shores. The Pitcher's thistle is extremely well adapted to a particular environment, the sand dunes. It is less prickly than other thistles, and the blue-green leaves, covered with fine white hairs, give the plant a downy, desert appearance. For thousands of years, it has coped with its environment, where nutrients are marginal and herbivores graze. The thistle takes six years to bloom, and then it dies and the seed disperses and starts again. This slow reproductive rate – combined with the fact that sand dunes everywhere are magnets for humans, erosion, and browsing white-tailed deer – has all but wiped them out. But here in Pukaskwa, the plant still stands a chance.

Ancient rock formations and huge rolling headlands with sheer cliffs and bald summits characterize the coast south to Cascade Falls. We passed the mouths of the White Gravel, White Spruce, and Swallow rivers, and tucked in behind the islands of small natural harbours at Nicols Cove, White Spruce Harbour, Simons Harbour, and English Fishery Harbour. The rolling rugged terrain is cut through with major ruptures or fault valleys. The layers of volcanic ash are kneaded and twisted, creating an incredible mosaic of colours and textures. Veins of quartz form stringy white patterns. On calm days like this, the green beds of lava intrusions reflect deep-sea colours, while the white sand beaches make the water Caribbean blue in shallow areas. When we closed our eyes, all we could hear were the gulls, loons, and white-throated sparrows.

Cascade Falls faces southwest, perfect for a shower at day's end. We all took turns, except Sila, climbing behind the curtain of water and sticking our heads out to feel the pounding spray massaging our backs. Later we walked the trail behind the cobble beach to see the upper falls. The view from here included Otter Island, where we were going the following day to visit another lighthouse.

The next morning, we paddled into the cove where the lighthouse keeper would have docked his boat. The three-storey building, with spacious rooms, including a big kitchen, was open, as it always is for travellers to use. Walkways lead out to the automated light, adorned with a beaver weathervane. Behind the island is *Nigi shtgwaaning*, Otterhead, a peninsula shaped naturally enough like an otter's head. It is one of the most exposed places on the entire Lake Superior shoreline – 400 kilometres (250 miles) of open water west-southwest to Duluth, Minnesota.

Imogene Cove is calm when we turn in towards the great sweep of beach. It is a place we have explored before. At the beach's east end, across Imogene Creek, is the site of a 1920s winter logging camp – Pukaskwa Depot. We pulled out a map hand-drawn by Lee Fletcher to show Ken and Rilla. Lee is now eighty-eight, but he was a boy when he lived here from 1920 to 1930 with his family. Ten years ago he sketched this layout of the depot for us, indicating where all the buildings had been: the Walking Boss's cabin, the Mills-Fletcher cabin (where he had lived), the depot office, the barn, the big bunkhouse, and the cookery. For thirteen years, from 1917 to 1930, the Pukaskwa Depot serviced the logging camps on the Julia, Ghost, Floating Heart, Pipe, and Imogene creeks, as well as the Pukaskwa. The people who lived at the depot included those with trades, such as the doctor, the harness-makers, and the blacksmith. The three hundred or so Scandinavian, Ojibwa, Scottish, but mostly French loggers who arrived by tug in the fall, with their horse teams and winter supplies, lived in the shanties built up the rivers, where they logged a mile or

The Cascade River's final plunge into Lake Superior makes for a wonderful natural shower. Pukaskwa National Park.

so in from either side of the water. Over the winter, they cut thirty thousand cords of spruce that they piled on the ice. In the spring, the cut logs descended the swollen rivers, scouring the banks as they tumbled out of the forest and into the lake. From here, a tug towed the boom south to a mill in Sault Ste. Marie. The isolation these people experienced is apparent even today, as this is the most remote section of the entire Great Lakes shoreline.

—◦—

At the Pukaskwa River's Schist Falls, Gary photographed the gorge of angular grey rock, beautifully lit. We camped on the gravel bar and enjoyed a most brilliant sunset. The next morning we were surprised to find that a porcupine had gnawed Ken and Rilla's leather pack straps until there was nothing left of them. We were thankful that it was not a trip with portages, and that the porcupine had eaten its fill of leather, not cedar wood. We followed the pigeon-toed tracks to the river, where they disappeared.

In two days we covered the stormy distance between the Pukaskwa River mouth and False Dog Harbour, where the shoreline is both intimidating and inviting. Michipicoten Island lay 25 kilometres (15 miles) to the south, a curving silhouette as enticing as Pic Island, only much larger and more remote. There are little sheltered coves along the mainland at Ganley Harbour, Redsucker Cove, and Floating Heart Bay, to name a few. Shoals and small islands provide some protection, but wherever the glacier-scarred shoreline is exposed to the open lake, the rock is laid bare to a height of 21 metres (70 feet) above the water before vegetation grows again. At the Flats, we made a commitment to the exposed stretch from Point Isacor across Tamarack Bay to the next safe haven.

False Dog Harbour's entrance was a welcome sight indeed. The relentless winds of this summer were building again, and we were on the verge of dangerous paddling conditions.

To reach the Dog River, we had only a short stretch of lake to paddle from False Dog Harbour. But even so, we knew the challenge could not be underestimated. The waves were still about a metre (3 feet) high. At first glance, the cobble beach at the river mouth appears like a wall. But on closer inspection, if one knows where to look, there is a place on the west side, where the river flows out into the lake through a channel wide enough for a canoe. We set up camp, leaving all our packs there. Then we proceeded upstream to one of Lake Superior's most spectacular watershed waterfalls, Denison Falls, where the low water had exposed fantastic kettle formations.

When we returned to our camp later that afternoon, the wind had died, but the sky was foretelling some serious weather. Through the crackle and static on our weather radio, we learned that another major storm was bearing down on the coast, with gale-force winds predicted for the following day. We decided to pack up and put a few more miles behind us. Off to the south, the silver path of a waxing moon glittered softly across the water while, in contrast, storm clouds looking purple even in the twilight piled up over the hills to the northeast. Our friends were some distance behind, but we all wore our headlamps to keep each other in sight. Gary navigated us safely to McCoy's Harbour, where we spent a fitful night awaiting the light.

The eastern horizon burned a sudden fiery crimson the next morning and we barely managed a quick departure before the rain. We pulled ahead of our friends several times in setting a stiff pace, and we were just resting, trying to decide if we should go on to the Michipicoten River or pull ashore at

Indian Beach, when a sudden wind decided for us. Even before landing on the beach, breaking waves were already dumping into our friends' uncovered canoe.

Where the current of the Michipicoten River met the rolling seas of Superior headlong, we stared in awe at the bay, now streaming with white combers. Water, wind, and waves pounded the cobbles and shaped the river mouth, a scene as mesmerizing now as it has been for all the thousands of travellers in the centuries before us.

Michipicoten Bay, August 17

For two years a plan has been brewing in Michipicoten Bay as dark and forbidding as the summer storm now engulfing it. It began when the Detroit-based road-building empire, the Carlos Companies Group, purchased a 1,000-acre (405 hectare) parcel of what was originally Algoma Central Railway land in Michipicoten Harbour and quietly began plans to operate an open-pit trap-rock mine on the shores of the bay. The change that it would make to life along this section of the Great Lakes Heritage Coast, with a mining venture stripping the forest and blasting, pulverizing, and shipping trap-rock to Michigan to make asphalt for building roads, is unimaginable. The Citizens Concerned for Michipicoten Bay requested that the Ontario government undertake an environmental assessment because of many factors, including the possibility of arsenic, a known carcinogen, carried in the clouds of dust produced by such an operation and the negative impact of noise and water pollution on important fish-spawning habitat in the bay. This scheme could set a precedent along the coast and undermine the spirit and intent of the entire Great Lakes

Heritage Coast program. Building a world-class, nature-based tourism economy depends on preserving the natural world and making sure the local economy is supported by this endeavour. In Northern Ontario, the cycle of a boom-and-bust economy caused by the extraction of natural resources has been the story for a long time. An economy based on enjoying and learning about the natural world without negatively exploiting it offers an alternative that most would agree is the ideal for this magnificent landscape. Michipicoten Bay is one of the finest gateways to the entire Great Lakes Heritage Coast. Now an essential quality needed is the willingness and imagination on the part of the local people and their municipal government to build a long-term, prosperous future for the region on something other than another resource-extraction enterprise in which the wealth ultimately leaves the land forever.

◄○►

Before travelling south, we paddled up the Michipicoten to visit the site of the old fur-trading post on the banks of the river. Beneath the surface, we could see the cribbing holding back the riverbank. It was here that the voyageur canoes tied up. Gary found a small clay pipe, a pipe stem, and some pieces of fine pottery sticking out of the riverbank. We left the canoe, climbed up the bank, and explored the various stone foundations, imagining life here 250 years ago at the height of the hustle-and-bustle fur trade. Until 1941, the Big House, the Hudson's Bay Company headquarters of the district, still stood here, containing hundreds of documents from the last days of the fur trade. Although the stores, warehouses, stables, residences, boat works, fish sheds, and tin smithy have vanished, archeologists have uncovered pewter, tiny blue teacups, earthenware, queen's ware, and decanters all carefully carried up

A profusion of mushrooms erupt from the sphagnum moss at the site of the longest-running Hudson's Bay Company depot on the Canadian shores of Lake Superior, just up the Michipicoten River.

from Montreal, now just in chips and fragments. The forest was returning, creeping across the fields and over the remnants of the fort, where pine seedlings, sumacs, and hawthorn flourished.

◄◊►

Three days later, we paddled into Old Woman Bay. We couldn't take our eyes off the two "old women," who peered out at us from those infamous dark cliffs. The rock here rises 200 metres (about 650 feet) straight up out of Lake Superior. Gnarly cedar, spruce, mosses, lichens, and rock textures framed and shaped the old women's features. By the time we reached the cobble beach, their faces had melded into plant and stone. It was here that we bid Ken, Rilla, and Oscar farewell until our next adventure together.

In the black cliffs of Bushy Bay, Cap Chaillon, and Grindstone Point, we saw silhouettes etched against the sky. The maze of cracks, crevices, and deep black caves were intriguing. From Grindstone Point to Ryan Point, we stopped occasionally to walk raised beaches, searching for Pukaskwa pits. In one such place, we counted more than forty of them. Monarch butterflies and hummingbirds flew out over the water, leaving the forest edge, which was shifting from the spruce and poplar of the boreal forest to that of the Great Lakes–St. Lawrence type: white and red pine, yellow birch, sugar maple, and white cedar.

By early evening, we had made some amazing progress by reaching Gargantua Harbour in just one day. Near the great throne of black basalt known as Nanabijou's Chair, cedar waxwings feasted on the evening insect life among the shoreline cedars. The view from here is breathtaking. You can see Michipicoten Island and Point Isacor 50 kilometres (30 miles) away to the west and northwest, and Leach Island en route to the Montreal River to the southeast. This enchanted landscape is filled with strange promontories and islands sculpted out of the porous volcanic rock. It is easy to imagine why this place held deep spiritual significance for the Ojibwa people.

On her belly, Sila slid out onto the bow deck of the canoe. Then she swung her legs down either side of the hull, sat up, and clasped the bow painter I had tied in a loop for reins. She rode the canoe over the waves as one would gallop a horse.

Around the point that shapes the south end of Katherine Cove lies one of the lake's greatest beaches, formed from sand carried down by the Sand (*Pinguisibi*) River. The counter-clockwise circulation of Lake Superior's waters, combined with wave action, has shaped the dunes over thousands of years. Dune grasses and beach pea plants both evolved with long root systems to hold the sand in place through the greatest storms. One monster storm had reshaped this coast as recently as the previous winter. All the way from Michipicoten Harbour, we

Balancing on beach logs

had observed the evidence – huge seas must have rushed upon the cliffs and over the headlands, uprooting trees and vegetation and revealing bedrock that had long been hidden.

The rock in this area was coloured white, grey, orange-pink, black, and green. Bands of quartz were shaped like tree-root systems squirming down the promontories. On the day we arrived at the Agawa Bay pictographs, we were fortunate to get in close to the lofty 30-metre (100-foot) cliff known as Inscription Rock to see the gallery of red ochre paintings. Enjoying them from the perspective of a canoe has been, and always will be, best, though more commonly people arrive by way of a steep trail and edge their way out along a smooth, angled ledge, hoping to avoid slipping into the lake. There are sea serpents, the horned lynx, the four moons, the caribou, and the many symbols of good hunting and safe journeys. But the most prominent paintings are of Missipeshu and Missikenahbik, two of the most respected of the Ojibwa manitous. Missikenahbik is at work when writhing squalls whip snakelike currents across the surface of the water or capture canoes uncertain in the serpentine currents off a point or a reef. When the clouds arch up in a series of ridges and the wind churns the lake to foam, it is Missipeshu, the horned lynx, swishing its ridge-backed tail. This sinister creature is also known as the child-stealer and the beach-stalker. We know from experience that they are very real depictions of Superior's most dangerous moods. Some pictographs are faded, some lie face down on the lake bottom, attached to chunks of cliff pried loose by winter frosts.

Our route took us past the Agawa River mouth, Agawa meaning "curve in the shore," or "shelter." At Agawa Bay, on a Saturday afternoon in August, it wasn't surprising to see numerous families playing in the water, digging in the sand, soaking up the sun, and climbing on the rocks at the end of the beach.

◄○►

Traversing the mouth of the Montreal River in a canoe can be treacherous if there is a strong onshore wind, because, as with the Michipicoten, the wind meets the outflowing current, creating waves stacked doubly high. In the bay to the south, we have friends, Ruth Fletcher and Ward Conway, who have anchored their lives to the rocks with the same kind of tenacity of the lichen, evolving and growing slowly over time. First, they built a log cabin, and then they added a shelter for wood, a workshop, guest quarters, a teepee, a sauna, pebble trails. The land has embraced them and shaped their lives. Our unannounced arrival surprised our friends, but the calm seas did not. Ward noted that it has become the pattern over fourteen years: whenever we come paddling by, the lake is always serene. And it happens to be the only way we can come ashore here, on these smooth, undulating rocks. I had told Sila stories about Ruth and Ward's cabin and about their two granddaughters, Sierra and Holly. So, although it was entirely coincidental to us that the girls were visiting and that the weather even allowed us to come ashore, it seemed perfectly natural to Sila that she should call out their names, that they should appear, and that she should simply step from the canoe she had been travelling in for the past six weeks and head off to play with them.

◄○►

It was Monday, and we had landed in Alona Bay between Theano Point and Pointe aux Mines to make our weekly 4:30 p.m. CBC Radio report. Sila was painting, Kalija was stretched out in the canoe's shade, Gary was looking at the map,

and I was talking with Gerald Graham, the host of the afternoon show in Thunder Bay. While on land, we knew the offshore wind had increased the size of the swells, but it was only possible to appreciate how big they were from previous experience. By the time we were halfway to Pointe aux Mines, the tarp was fastened and Sila was sitting between my legs facing the waves, a smile on her face. Kalija's head rested on my seat and her eyes were closed. Never had we known a summer as windy as this one.

These points along the eastern shore of Lake Superior are rich with minerals. By the mid-1800s, Pointe aux Mines, Mica Bay, and Coppermine Point had all attracted organized mining. Pits, head frames, tailings, and shantytowns popped up everywhere and had an unhealthy effect on the water, fish, and animals. The aboriginal people, feeling bewildered and angry, protested the disregard for their homeland, but by now there was too much momentum to turn the tide, and too much get-rich-quick money to be made from the Earth's resources. The legacy of mine waste sites in Northern Ontario continuing to this day is testimony to this approach that has so often left the north impoverished.

At this point, the shoreline begins its turn towards the lake's most easterly point at Old Mill Bay. A huge wetland forms the area between Hibbard Bay and Sawpit Bay, and then the topography rises to a hill around which we navigated into Pancake Bay, named for its round, flat shape. Most of the 4-kilometre (2.5-mile)-long beach here is part of a popular provincial park. In the days of the fur trade, this was an easy 50-kilometre (30-mile) trip from Sault Ste. Marie for canoes that would regularly cover twice that distance daily.

◄○►

Playing with our evening shadows on the canvas tarpaulin was similar to our finger-shadow puppet show on the tent wall at night with flashlights.

As we paddled into Batchawana Bay, instead of following the shoreline, we made a beeline to Batchawana Island, a large, low, flat island that lies centred in the bay. We have many memories of visiting this island through the seasons. One February evening, when the ice was all smooth, we donned our skates at shore, and they carried us gliding, circling, spinning, and flying in a 15-kilometre (9-mile) loop from Harmony Beach to Batchawana Island to Havilland Bay and back. An unforgettable view of the landscape we call Home.

◄○►

We left Batchawana Bay on the hottest day of the summer. Sweat poured off us, stinging our eyes, soaking our backs. To keep Kalija cool, I tied a water-soaked hat to her head. Sila slept soundly, draped over the bow deck like a rag doll. The coast of Batchawana Bay and around the Goulais Peninsula across Goulais Bay was completely different from the shoreline so far. Despite the exposure to Superior's westerly winds, the cedar and mountain ash trees grow right to the water's edge, softening the rugged look of the land. The beautiful, flat, cream-and-red-coloured Jacobsville sandstone, rare in Ontario, forms a shallow shelf out in the lake. This acts as a barrier, causing the surf to break up long before it reaches shore. Ile Parisienne and the North and South Sandy islands appeared on this hazy afternoon to be far more distant than they really were. During October, the trout spawn in the shoals surrounding these islands, and many ducks and geese use the protected waters for breeding, feeding, and nesting.

We paddled straight across Goulais Bay, taking advantage of the calm evening. To the east, the Goulais River flowed out of the Algoma Highlands. The meandering lower reaches of the river through the pastoral Goulais Valley and the river mouth provide an important habitat for a myriad of bird species from warblers to owls to ducks, geese, and eagles.

At the promontory of Gros Cap, the clear turquoise waters surged against black basaltic cliffs. Beneath our canoe, far below the surface, boulders of many shapes and colours patterned the lake bottom at the entrance to Whitefish Bay. Offshore lie the Gros Cap Reefs, indicated by an enormous channel marker. Beyond lies the dredged shipping lane following the international boundary between Canada and the United States. This commercial transportation route linking the Lakehead with the St. Lawrence throbs with the beat of diesel-engine power carrying products west and resources east.

The St. Mary's River, September 3

As we paddled towards the international bridge arching over the St. Mary's River between Sault Ste. Marie, Ontario, and Sault Ste. Marie, Michigan, Sila waved to the occupants of cars and trucks strung out bumper to bumper, waiting to cross the border. For those waving back, we were a distraction from the modern-day frustration of being stuck in traffic on a beautiful afternoon.

The St. Mary's River is one of the most historic rivers in Canada, and lies at the geological crossroads of the continent. The river physically links three of the Great Lakes – Superior, Huron, and Michigan – and it is the most important ecological and hydrological link within the heart of North America. Two hundred years ago, our route downriver would have been via the Whitefish Rapids around Whitefish Island. The rapids were once one of the most productive habitats for fish on the North American continent, with whitefish being the most abundant –

and the most delectable to eat and preserve by smoking and drying. Because of them, the aboriginal people established settlements on the islands more than five thousand years ago. Whitefish Island was once one of the largest pre-European settlements in the upper Great Lakes. Nineteenth-century writer and traveller Anna Jameson described the experience of paddling through here in her wonderful book *Winter Studies and Summer Rambles in Canada*.

The St. Mary's River was also part of the transcontinental fur-trade route that encouraged the movement of Europeans westwards. As modern travellers entering the Sault Canal on this harnessed and industrialized river, we could only imagine the long portage upstream or the thrilling whitewater descent of long ago. On the Canadian side of the river, the locks are part of a national historic site. We paddled into the locks and watched the huge doors swing shut behind us. Once we discovered what a great echo chamber we were in, we filled it with the sounds of loon calls and wolf howls. A simple gravity-feed system lowered us 6.5 metres (22 feet), the majority of the river's drop to Lake Huron. Afterwards, folks from Parks Canada, along with Sault Ste. Marie's mayor, other dignitaries, friends, and well-wishers, greeted us at the lock's large brownstone headquarters.

Since the mayor, the tourism director, and the federal member of parliament were present, it appeared that the Great Lakes Heritage Coast program was being embraced by the city. Our journey was helping to gain the general public's attention. In a city largely built upon an industrial economy, where the resources of the land have always been seen to be most valuable when they are harvested, mined, harnessed, or captured, people are only just grasping the idea that this natural landscape, unique in the world, can have much greater long-term value.

At this point, we sadly said goodbye to Kalija when our Goulais River friends Robin and Enn offered to take her for the duration of our journey. We knew she would be happy no longer having to endure the unusual late-summer heat and humidity.

◄○►

We pressed close to the Canadian shore, following the curving river north of Sugar Island. Over the next few days, our route would take us south down Lake George, through the islands of the St. Joseph Channel, and out into the North Channel of Lake Huron. The landscape had flattened out, and we noticed again how the forest had changed. The beech, white ash, and chestnut were now growing up amongst the more familiar shoreline species of cedar, spruce, balsam, birch, and pine. Sandhill cranes circled. Ten- to fifteen-pound salmon — chinook, coho, and pink — were on the move, returning to spawning places in the rivers that flow to Lake Huron, including the St. Mary's. Sila climbed out on the bow to watch for them. The sudden surprise of churning, cloudy waters, the splash of a wide tail fin near the canoe, or a leaping fish made her laugh out loud.

On a misty morning threatening rain we saw a large flock of cormorants on Lake George. Their ravenous appetite, and perhaps their black serpentine appearance, has made them targets of unwarranted persecution. Through the 1960s and 1970s, their thinning eggshells and deformed chicks with twisted beaks were held up as examples of the effects of toxic pollution. In recent years, declining fish stocks have been blamed on the cormorants, though there has never been a credible scientific study done to prove this matter. The double-crested cormorants are not foreign invaders like some species, but they do feed largely on two invaders: alewives and smelt, which expand with the depletion of larger sport fish. We must be careful not to make the cormorant a scapegoat for a changing ecosystem that humans have affected more than all other species combined.

We camped on the islands beneath white pine on bedrock opposite Richards Landing, to the squawk of blue herons in a nearby bay, the high-pitched cry of osprey, and the vigorous hammering of a pair of pileated woodpeckers. Farther east, as we left the delta of islands and entered the North Channel, a variety of smaller gulls and terns dipped and dove over the web of beautiful shoals that we wove carefully through on our way to the Mississagi Delta. Near Thessalon, we paddled close to a congregation of fifty loons, gathering for fall migration. One evening, a honking V-formation of Canada geese flew low over our tent. We felt their size by the vibration of their powerful wing beats.

Lake Huron's North Channel, September 6

Lake Huron, including Georgian Bay, is the second-largest Great Lake and, globally, the third-largest expanse of freshwater. Of all the Great Lakes, Lake Huron has the longest shoreline and more islands than any other lake in the world. And Manitoulin is the largest island on any freshwater lake on Earth.

Between Thessalon and Blind River, we paddled along a shoreline of small, sandy coves, low headlands and points bounded by white pine with treed wetlands and marshes. We were careful not to scrape our canoe hull against the rocks as we paddled through the extensive shallows and shoals. Amidst the near-shore islands, warm reed beds provided shelter and

Part of the excitement of a long journey is the new view from the tent door every morning.

food for numerous ducks and geese. This was a great paddler's paradise, since it would always be too treacherous for any kind of motorized craft.

Wetlands have a subtle beauty all their own. Travelling slowly and quietly with binoculars always at hand, we were amazed at the flocks of black ducks, mallards, and teal amongst the white water lilies, bulrushes, sedges, and cattails.

In Bruce Mines, we were jarred by the sounds of a busy industrial port. The hill that once framed the community lakeshore was now being blasted, processed, and shipped away. White noise, rock crushing, the sound of gigantic vehicles on the move – this gave some idea of what the planned trap-rock mine in Michipicoten Bay would be like, as we thought back to that pristine landscape.

Just prior to reaching the Mississagi Delta, we stopped for lunch and a swim on the inside of Hennepin Island. To the north of us were the wetlands of Mississagi Bay, an important staging and breeding area for sandhill cranes. Through here, Sila pointed out the strange "gulls" with blood-red bills skimming across the surface – the Caspian terns.

For thousands of years a classic "bird's foot" delta has been forming at the mouth of the Mississagi on Lake Huron. With its shifting channels and low, flat islands, this delta is one of the best examples of its kind on the Canadian Great Lakes, and it has long supported human settlement. To the Ojibwa, this is *Miswezaging*, "the river of many mouths." A Hudson's Bay Company post and cemetery were once located here, and at the abandoned Sayer farmstead, there are now wild fields and huge lilac bushes. Today, the land above the riverbank on the eastern side of the delta has been cleared for a golf course and a uranium refinery.

The Mississagi was the place where we had planned to meet the film crew from CBC-TV's popular, nationally televised program *On the Road Again*. Many scenes were shot from different perspectives, requiring three or four takes, and I was astonished at Sila's patience. In one scene, we were paddling down the West Branch, with Sila looking over the bow and the cameraman filming forward, when a black bear swam across the river in front of us. How fortunate was that!

◄○►

The town of Blind River officially welcomed us at the marine park, where a modern windmill generates energy. A community that develops such ecological infrastructure has more capital in the long term for other projects, such as the hiking trails planned between the communities of Blind River and Spanish. The town council, a group of high-school students, community members, and tourists attended. I was particularly happy to see the young people from a Grade 12 economics class. For those who love their "homeland" on the North Channel, there are employment opportunities if they have imagination, entrepreneurial skills, and a willingness to design their own field of work.

◄○►

Our canoe seemed to carve a path through the fog and humidity. A storm was brewing. Swirling mare's tails and cirrus clouds patterned the dark, looming, thundery atmosphere. At Algoma Mills, the winds suddenly picked up, and we made it into Bootlegger's Bay in the nick of time. We snapped on the canoe cover and raced for the shelter of the forest. Great cracks of lightning and pelting rain deluged us, and then moved past quickly. Later that day, a strong tailwind gave us a grand ride through the Whale's Back Channel.

Some of the larger, offshore islands are buff-coloured limestone, others like the Benjamin Islands in Fox Harbour are formed of pink and red granite. In the Benjamin Islands, we had our first glimpse of Manitoulin Island to the south and the La Cloche Mountains to the north. Rising dramatically above the North Channel, these white quartzite ridges are sparsely covered by white pine, red pine, Jack pine, and red oak. On the lower slopes, closer to the shoreline where the soil is deeper, sugar maple grow with beech and cherry trees. Little splashes of red and yellow in the maples, birches, and sumac indicated the change in season, despite the warm days. There was a continuous chirp of crickets. Over the course of the trip, Sila had been picking little bouquets of flowers for the tent. They were now bunches of autumn flowers – goldenrod, purple asters, and pearly everlasting. Darkness came earlier, giving us time for "stargazing," an endlessly fascinating occupation. Over the next few days, we paddled close to the ancient quartzite mountains down into Bay of Islands and the La Cloche Peninsula.

One particular night the terrain of every island we stopped at was sloped, wavy, or lumpy. A tortured surface of egg-carton limestone and brown granite, cut deeply with fissures, cracks, and holes, made finding a campsite all but impossible. It was getting late and, suitable or not, we finally stopped a short paddle from the community of Birch Island. A half-moon rose to the east while a band of cerise-coloured clouds hung just over the La Cloche Mountains. The only sounds were those of fish surfacing to feed with a gentle plop, plop, plop, the trumpeting of sandhill cranes, the crickets, and a pair of young beavers slapping their tails on the water.

At the narrows in the La Cloche Channel, with Birch Island to our east, we saw the first big layers of limestone shoreline reminiscent of the Niagara Escarpment, a glacial deposit that extends south for 1,000 kilometres (600 miles). Dreamer's Rock, the nub of quartzite on the southern tip of the La Cloche Peninsula, has long been a place of spiritual significance to the local aboriginal people. Indeed, an elderly native woman appeared to be involved in a healing ceremony when we arrived. Someone was wrapped in a blanket lying on a platform. The elder was bent over this figure, speaking in Ojibwa. We did not portage our canoe across the isthmus, but carried on around the peninsula, not wanting to be intrusive. For centuries, vision quests, fasts, ceremonies, and powwows have taken place here.

With the wind to our backs, we traversed Frazer Bay and made for Killarney Harbour. It was a long day for all of us. While paddling up the channel between Badgely Island and Badgely Point, we passed an abandoned quarry on one side and an active quarry on the other. This region has a long history of extracting quartzite. Some 9,500 years ago, when

Sila investigating a fresh beaver cut in a red oak

the Great Lakes water levels were higher, Paleo-Indians were living here, quarrying this stone for tools. For thousands of years, the people chipped away at the hills, leaving little evidence of their work. However, in the past fifty years, entire hills have been quarried. They have disappeared forever, transformed into silica dioxide and loaded onto cargo ships bound for southern Ontario and Michigan for the making of glass, steel, and glass cookware. There is a finite amount of rock to carry away, and once it is gone, what do the local people mine? What does a community do with a shoreline made ugly by industrial activity?

◄○►

It was spitting rain and getting dark by the time we paddled into Killarney Harbour. An array of yachts, smaller sailboats, and powerboats were either tied up in the slips or had been pulled out of the water for the season. We paddled by the general store and various outfitting lodges. Then we saw the sign for Killarney Mountain Lodge. Earlier in the year, Jennifer East, whose family owns the lodge, had invited us to stop in. As preparations unfolded, the lodge proved an ideal place for picking up the sixth of our seven supply packages. Maury and Annabelle East, Jennifer's parents, gave us a wonderful welcome that evening and provided us with a cabin out of the rain, a place to recharge spirits and our batteries, organize photographs and stories, and refill our packs with food for the journey to Killbear Provincial Park. We learned how an elaborate program of activities that involved day trips and overnight adventures to explore the region had sustained the lodge for thirty years.

While we were at the lodge, a group of thirteen artists arrived to paint. This landscape has inspired some of Canada's most famous painters. Tom Thomson's striking style captures Georgian Bay's wind-twisted pine trees and rocky shore in famous canvases such as *The West Wind*. In the 1930s, Group of Seven artist A.Y. Jackson arrived in Killarney. While canoeing into the interior, Jackson was struck by the rugged grandeur of snow-white mountains amidst northern forests and lakes. He renamed Trout Lake OSA Lake after the Ontario Society of Artists. His endeavour to protect the beauty of the landscape stirred up enough political will to have the region designated as Killarney Provincial Park.

Georgian Bay, September 17

It was our first frosty morning as we left Killarney Harbour, passing the red rock at the southern entrance. The wind, not long quiet, picked up, urging us into the protection of Collins Inlet north of Philip Edward Island. Numerous fishing boats were trolling in the inlet's cloudy waters.

Beaverstone Bay marked the beginning of the navigational challenge of Georgian Bay's famed Thirty Thousand Islands. This Precambrian Shield rock, scoured clean by the glaciers, forms a multitude of low islands and shoals that actually number three times thirty thousand. Grey granite islands and finger-shaped shoals created a labyrinth of possible routes. At the mouth of the French River, the trees and plants growing at the shoreline were stunted and windswept. Scrub juniper and blueberries and gnarled, twisted trunks of white pine, Jack pine, and cedar struggled to grow in the thin, sparse pockets of soil.

In 1983, when we had paddled out of the mouth of the French River en route to the Arctic Ocean, we were following the same route travelled by the voyageurs, fur traders, and explorers – French and English. French-Canadian voyageurs, exploiting the continent for its fur-bearing animals like the beaver, were part of a vast inland empire based in Montreal. They adapted the aboriginal birchbark canoes by building large ones – 11 metres (36 feet) long – to carry trade goods and supplies into the North American interior and to bring the furs out.

The mouth of the French River fans out into three major outlets: the Western Outlet, the Voyageur Channel, and the Main Outlet. Outside this river mouth on Georgian Bay, there are hundreds of islands, and the channels between them form a veritable maze. Some are wide, others just allowed our canoe to pass. Others looked promising but proved to be dead ends. A little mink swam across in front of the canoe. We followed it for a while, as it skittered along. We were spending longer days in the canoe, realizing that this spell of warm weather may suddenly end.

From Henvey Inlet south to Pointe au Baril, the jagged 30-kilometre (18-mile) coastline included the important Naiscoot River wetlands. On our topographic map, of the thousands of shoals, only those farthest from shore were named: Sophia Rock, McHugh Rock, Red Rock, and Norgate Rocks. Coming across steam boilers, the only surviving remains from shipwrecked steamers, was part of the journey through here. Georgian Bay is a place of bliss or peril, depending on the weather, the boater's navigational skills – and sometimes just fate. Beneath us, the rock was striped with a swirling pattern of black-and-pink ribbons. The relentless wind kept blowing, exhausting us as much from the stress of anticipating a crash-landing as from the exertion of paddling against it.

Twisting our torsos and using our entire bodies to propel the canoe forward, we were able to make headway towards Norgate Inlet. Waves striking the reefs sent spray in all directions, making the job of reading the water almost impossible. Suddenly, I planted my paddle into an underwater crack, where it stuck firm. This was followed by the sickening sound of splintering wood. In the shock, I let go. The paddle stood bolt upright as the canoe sailed past it. Gary grabbed it, yanking sharply upwards. Luckily the laminations of cherry and ash held strong, and I was able to snap the tip back straight, and the paddle served well for the rest of the voyage.

Still rattled from the paddle experience, I failed to see a large band of black rock until it was too late. I could hear the scraping sound run the entire length of the canoe. Gary smiled at me and angled the canoe towards an island just south of Burritts Bay. "Let's take a break, Joanie."

I held the canoe while Sila climbed out. Then Gary pulled the bow up to rest in a neat hollow of rock. We collapsed on the warm ground and stared upwards at the flat, grey sky. It had

been a stressful morning. A Monarch butterfly flew past, also struggling against the wind. I immediately felt humbled. We were going only as far as Port Severn. This delicate creature was heading for Mexico.

In shallow depressions where water pooled, we inspected thick sponges of moss and discovered plump, wild cranberries. Just south of here, the Gibson First Nation have made a successful business out of growing cranberries commercially. Over a period of years, they have reconstructed the bogs to grow the berry once common to this landscape.

Paddling through Bayfield Inlet gave us the first indication as to how challenging it might be to find a place to camp from here to Port Severn. Everywhere there was a cottage and a dock. Most of the land was privately owned. Big boats zoomed up the Alexander Passage. How much human flotsam ends up in the lake? we wondered. Oil and gas from marinas and boats, septic leakage from cottages. Construction and shoreline development goes on and on, moving northward.

It was nearly nightfall and, as luck would have it, we found a suitable island on which to camp. Gary went for a quick swim in a nearby cove, then called us over. A water snake was slithering up onto shore from the lake, also seeking shelter for the night. With great blue herons, eagles, ospreys, otters, coyotes, foxes, raccoons, northern pike, and muskies hunting snakes from the air, the land, and the water, it must have been a challenging existence indeed on a bare rock landscape.

◄○►

We celebrated the fall equinox under stormy autumn skies in the company of longtime locals Heather Dale McLaren and sixty-five-year-old Emmaline Madigan. Emmaline welcomed us to the Pointe au Baril lighthouse, where her married life began at age seventeen and where she raised six children. One of the many photographs adorning the walls of the lighthouse is of her children boarding the School Boat in September 1958. She herself was schooled on School House Island near Pointe au Baril Harbour. She was the only woman, and last lighthouse keeper, in a line of seven that dated back to the first posting by Samuel Oldfield in 1889. We climbed narrow stairs to the now-automated light. Once, Emmaline's nightly ritual had been the lighting of a kerosene lantern. To the west, the steel-grey waters of Georgian Bay rolled in. To the east was Steamboat Channel and the dilapidated, red-roofed Bellevue Hotel. Behind those boarded windows, we imagined the "swing era," ghosts still dancing to the music of the 1920s, when steamships plied the waters dropping passengers at the grand resort.

Killbear Provincial Park, September 25

When Gary's parents applied to the Ontario government in the 1940s to purchase a beautiful sand bay west of Parry Sound, the only one of its kind on Georgian Bay, they were declined. The surveyors' report indicated to the government that this was a very special place, which should remain public. It later became Killbear Provincial Park.

◄○►

Sila walked quietly up to Kenton Otterbein's side, her attention glued to the 1-metre(3-foot)-long fox snake coiling around his arm like a ribbon of gold-and-black diamonds. She held out her hands, gently taking the constrictor, which now hung down towards her like a rope. I watched the eager, entranced faces of the elementary-age students as Killbear Park's head naturalist

In Killbear Provincial Park, Sila holds a captive-born eastern fox snake. The Greater Georgian Bay Reptile Awareness program <www.gbayreptiles.com> is successfully educating people about Ontario's endangered reptiles, of which this constrictor is one.

A lunch break in the Georgian Bay Islands

explained how these snakes swim up to 5 kilometres (3 miles) from the mainland to hibernate on distant islands. He held up a small hutch. Behind the Plexiglas panel, the students could see a small, reclusive creature – Ontario's only poisonous reptile, the eastern massasauga rattlesnake. Other rare reptiles in the region include the eastern fox snake, the eastern hognose snake, the five-lined skink, the spotted turtle, the wood turtle, and the Blanding's turtle. Slowly but surely, the park's Greater Georgian Bay Reptile Awareness Program is helping to preserve these threatened species, which have long been persecuted by humans. After making a short presentation about our voyage and answering a barrage of questions from the students, we got back into the canoe. Sila stood at the bow waving to the students as we paddled off, heading south towards Massasauga Provincial Park.

Each day we found new signs of how far south our route had taken us. In Killbear, Sila collected beechnuts along with acorns. Crows, not ravens, awoke us one morning at a campsite on McCrae Lake near Beausoleil Island. A hum of distant traffic reminded us we were within 8 kilometres (5 miles) of a major highway linking south and north, a highway that is only getting wider, straighter, faster, eating up wetlands whose disappearance will mean the demise of many species, especially the endangered rattlesnakes.

The geology of Georgian Bay was one of the most interesting aspects of our travel in the last leg of our voyage. The metamorphic rock is moulded, layered, striped, smooth, orange, black, beige, and white. The paddling conditions had never been more varied, and the human pressures on the coastal ecosystem had never been more evident than in this last week of our journey, from Parry Sound to Port Severn. Amidst these heavily used and privately owned lands, even the smallest Muskoka Heritage Areas and Conservation Reserves represent important natural habitat protection.

The contrast between the wilderness of the First Nation lands around Moose Point and the cottage developments is stark. On a lovely September Saturday north of Honey Harbour, we found ourselves on the "Highway 401" of waterways, dodging boat wakes, wondering at a landscape so completely transformed in the twenty-two years since we last paddled this way. The water was quite clean back then. Now, in places, it is no longer fit for swimming, let alone drinking. Islands that for years supported a single cottage were now subdivided into a dozen lots. Entire species of fish are under extreme pressure. And with the accelerated pace and the loss of nature's peace and serenity, it seems wilderness recedes both physically and spiritually. What was happening here put everything else we experienced on this journey in perspective.

Perhaps one day a designated Water Trail will thread its way through these islands, encouraging more people to step into a canoe or kayak or non-motorized vessel to enjoy what is fast becoming an endangered environment. The leadership provided by the local concerned citizens devising conservation initiatives is encouraging. The Georgian Bay Association, the Greater Bay Area Foundation, and the Georgian Bay Land Trust are working hard on many environmental projects with the cottagers and the boaters. With limited time left, they recognize that everyone will have to work together for the protection of what remains of this unique ecosystem. Protection of the coastal ecosystems must be the number-one goal everywhere along the Great Lakes Heritage Coast.

Among the Thirty Thousand Islands, there lies a tiny national park, established in 1929 to protect a portion of this landscape from private ownership. Georgian Bay Islands National Park is just 12 square kilometres (4.5 square miles) in size, taking in all or parts of the fifty-nine islands spread out along the southeast shore of Georgian Bay. Only four islands are accessible to the public – Beausoleil, Centennial, Bone, and Island 95. Of these, Beausoleil Island is the largest, and the focal point of park activities and services. The north end of the island is glacier-scraped rock, with windswept pines bent and twisted on the exposed shoreline. The southern part of Beausoleil is dominated by tall hardwood forests and thick, rich soils, where hundreds of species of plants and animals and a variety of reptiles and amphibians reside, including the eastern massasauga rattlesnake. The life that this national park represents and protects never seemed more fragile as humanity's all-pervasive influence inundates our senses day and night.

A family reflection in a pool along the north shore

REFLECTIONS AT THE JOURNEY'S END

Severn Sound, September 30

The fall season was stirring in all of nature now. Sila pointed out the loons wearing their grey-and-white winter plumage. Mirages turned islands "upside down" in the distance and told us that, despite the continued warm weather, Georgian Bay was cooling down. We watched otters eating freshwater clams. A white-tailed doe and her fawn swam across our path in Severn Sound. After the exhausting buzz of human activity, we felt comforted by the peaceful scene.

Sila reached out to touch each green or red buoy up the last stretch of the Waubaushene Channel, as if she were completing a connect-the-dots puzzle. Marsh grasses swayed gently on either side of the canoe. A pair of whistling swans glided regally through the shoals and wetlands like a couple of tiny ships. The sky was blue. In our mind's eye we returned to the beginning of our voyage at Pigeon Bay, named for the passenger pigeon whose kind once blackened these skies at this time of the year. We imagined flocks of birds so great they cast a shadow on the land like a passing cloud. Their extinction through hunting was shocking, because it seemed to happen so suddenly. But those birds depended upon a population base of a certain size for survival, and when the population dipped below the critical mass, it plummeted quickly. We thought of the Great Lakes Heritage Coast and the ways humanity is gnawing away at the ecosystems. These coastal systems are self-sustaining, but, like the passenger pigeon, their numbers are dwindling. The incremental loss of self-sustaining coastal habitats could add up one day to complete loss, and we will be surprised, as we are in many places, that wilderness and its wildlife is gone forever. We hope that people's strong attachment to their special places along the coast will take precedence, so that they adopt long-term visions of protection.

As individuals, our influence can be great. But we have to believe we can make a difference. While we cannot rely on our governments to act in the best interest of nature, we can do everything to encourage them in that direction. We can either drift like little clouds – or we can be the storm of change. We are the weather. Encouraging environmental education and adopt-a-place programs in our school systems are an inspiring way to teach many people while building a sense of responsibility for one's own backyard. We can live healthier lives at home and in the workplace, and by doing so each of us becomes an example to inspire others. At this time and place in the history of the planet, our species has never had greater influence. We won't have a second chance. There is no other shoreline like this on the Earth.

THE JOURNEY IN PICTURES

Spar Island

Orange lichen

This cluster of Orange Earth Tongues, Microglossum rufum, *is growing, characteristically, among mosses in rich humus. We have always found this mushroom to be yellow, not orange.*

These small, brightly coloured mushrooms, Hygrophorus miniatus, *are one of the two hundred species of Waxy Caps.*

Morning light near Tee Harbour beneath the Sleeping Giant cliffs

It is our luck to catch this seasonal highlight of the Sleeping Giant: the profusion of flowering blue flags, wild irises, in the lowland bogs.

From the top of Ontario's highest vertical cliffs, we enjoy an expansive view of our "crossing" from Pie Island to Thunder Cape.

A view from the Sleeping Giant overlooking part of the proposed Lake Superior National Marine Conservation Area, the fourth in Canada

A reflection at Teepee Harbour

The view from an overlook at Squaw Harbour is of Bowman Island and, in the distance, St. Ignace Island.

Daisies fluttering gaily at the MacKay's Harbour campsite brought back sunny memories of several trips here over the course of many years.

A profusion of spruce cones clustered on the forest floor is an essential year-round food for the red squirrel.

In these islands, the places that are appealing to pull ashore now are usually places where people have camped for thousands of years.

In Morn Harbour, drifting smoke from a distant forest fire darkened the sky to an earthy colour, like an ominous storm brewing.

Twin flowers in full bloom

Terraced beaches are one of our favourite types of campsites along Lake Superior's north shore.

The Battle Island lighthouse has been operating for 125 years and, although it is now fully automated, the lighthouse keeper still lives here five months of the year.

The lighthouse keeper recounted how a 1977 November gale, with monstrous seas and a roaring wind, smashed the lantern glass 120 feet above the lake.

Generations of travellers have paddled through these tranquil islands, which have always held great spiritual significance for the aboriginal people.

South side of Wilson Island

The stromatolites found near Flint Island in Schreiber Channel are an example of a fossilized blue-green algae colony, the Earth's earliest oxygen-breathing life forms.

Schreiber Channel

Harebells grow in the crevasses of bare bedrock islands along with other subarctic plants that flourish in the cool microclimate created by the lake.

Twin Harbours in Collingwood Bay

Despite the hot days, many evenings on Lake Superior were cool enough for a campfire made with small pieces of drift we found along the shore.

The Slates are an island archipelago most noted for the fluctuating population of woodland caribou.

Driftwood and stones on the beach, Slate Islands

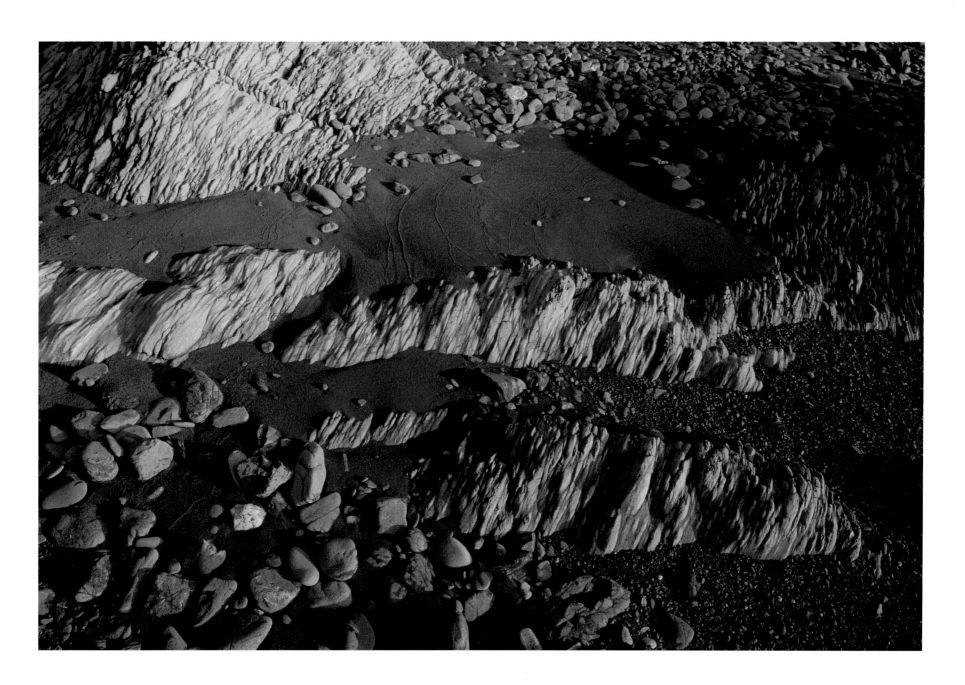

The rocks on the Slate Islands are intriguing to all for the patterns and colours.

Bits of driftwood gathered near the Little Pic River

McGreevey Harbour, Slate Islands

This cushion plant, a sphagnum moss, was growing in profusion, cascading down the bank to the water's edge on Patterson Island.

Ornate-stalked bolete, a fleshy fungi that has pores instead of gills on the underside of the cap

Ripened bunchberries provide an important fall food for mice, squirrels, grouse, and white-tailed deer.

Clubmoss

A windy sky foretells a weather change. Sure enough, it rained the next morning.

The Coldwell Peninsula

Prisoner's Cove, Neys Provincial Park

Peninsula Bay, Detention Island, Pic Island, and the Coldwell Peninsula

Sunset over Pic Island

Three pools on Foster Island

A Woodland caribou was waiting out the wind just as we were.

The rolling surf became a common sight during the unusually windy summer.

Whenever we brought the canoe ashore, we rested it on two canvas-covered pads to protect the wood hull.

Foster Island and the Coldwell Peninsula along Lake Superior's north shore

Pebble Beach

The sound of chattering rocks rolled around by the waves is as intriguing a sensation as the feel of one of them in your hands.

Shoreline rocks, Marathon

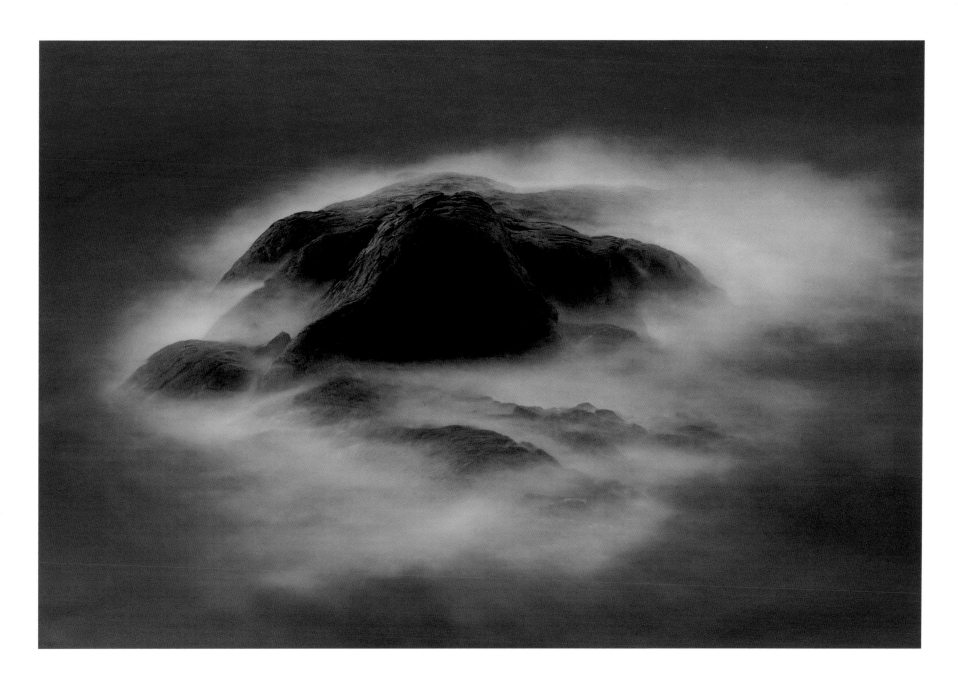

Offshore reef, Campbell Point near Hattie Cove

Glass-smooth and slippery, this golden rock north of Hattie Cove was unlike anything we had seen before.

Fireweed in Cardon Cove

Sand beach south of Pic River

Waves sculpting an ever-changing pattern on the beach at Oiseau Bay

The White River flowing through Pukaskwa National Park is the best year-round whitewater river on the east side of Lake Superior.

Flowing water at Chigamiwinigum Falls, White River

Morrison Harbour

We spend one windbound day with our friends Ken and Rilla exploring up the White River between Lake Superior and Chigamiwinigum Falls.

Gliding over the unbelievably clear water along the Pukaskwa Coast

Near Gids Harbour, Pukaskwa Coast

Cascade Falls, Pukaskwa National Park

Cascade River

Birchbark patterns

Flying our kite on a windbound day at Imogene Bay

Wave patterns over sand, Imogene River

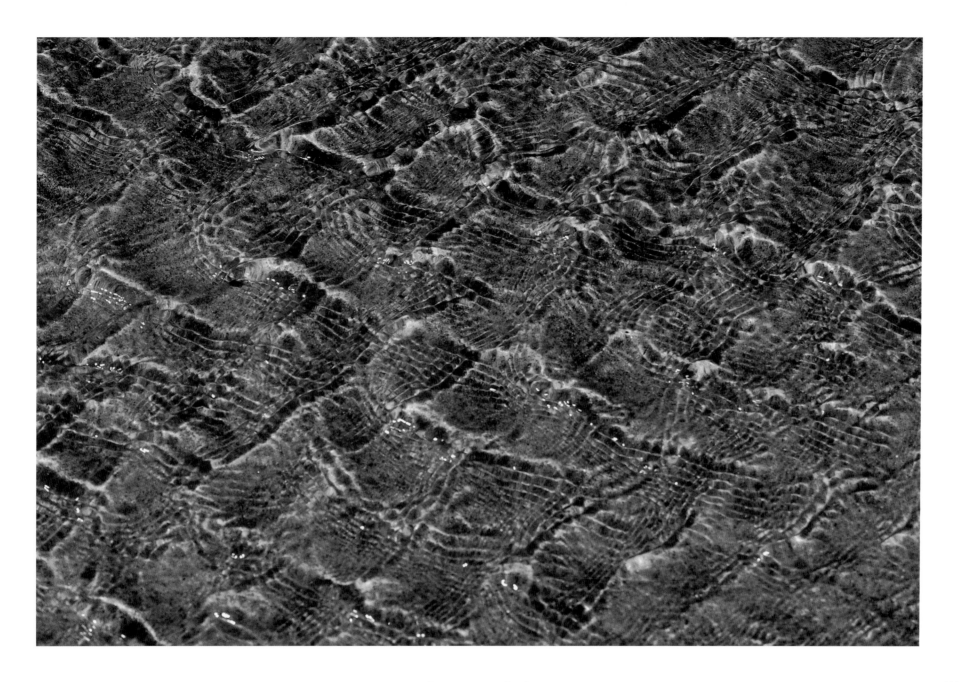

Water flowing over sand, Julia River

Campbell Creek

Floating Heart Bay was an oasis at the end of a long day's paddle from the Pukaskwa River.

Rocks at False Dog Harbour

Denison Falls, Dog River

The view from False Dog Harbour looking east towards distant Michipicoten Bay

The Great Lakes hold the largest volume of freshwater on the planet, and Lake Superior is the greatest expanse of this precious substance.

Driftwood faces

A kettle formation on the Dog River

Water-sculpted rock on the Dog River

Low water in late summer reveals the rock structure beneath the Dog River's Denison Falls

Nanabijou's Chair at Gargantua

Gargantua, Lake Superior Provincial Park

Robertson Cove

Tugboat Channel

Larry Island, North Channel of Lake Huron near Thessalon

White water lilies

Lichens, grasses, mosses on granite rock

Fox Island, McBean Channel

The Benjamin Islands, North Channel of Lake Huron

Pink granite, Benjamin Islands

North Channel of Lake Huron west of the La Cloche Mountains

Wind-twisted pine of the North Channel

White pine emerging from the morning fog on the North Channel

Bay of Islands near the La Cloche Mountains, North Channel

Beaverstone Bay on Georgian Bay

Sunset reflection south of Henvey Inlet, Georgian Bay

A pool of water lying in a smooth rock depression on Black Bay gives the appearance of an arch.

Bedrock shoals with the Bustard Islands on the horizon

Glacier-scoured rock, Elm Tree Island, Bayfield Inlet

Intrusions of black lava snake through the metamorphic rocks near Wreck Island, Georgian Bay.

Sunset at Sand Bay on Georgian Bay

Frosty tamarack at dawn, late September

Travelling in the protection of islands north of Pointe au Baril enabled us to make progress despite days of constant wind in Georgian Bay's Thirty Thousand Islands.

McCrae Lake near journey's end

Acknowledgements

The "environment" is no further away than our next breath, and so it is odd that we toss it around like a political football, wondering whose responsibility it is to look after "it." "It" is nothing less than ourselves and the intrinsic link we have with every living thing. The following organizations are only several of many incredible ones whose work helps us to "think globally and act locally." Curbing our appetites, improving our habits, and taking action are within the realm of possibility for us all if we love ourselves, our children, and wish a future for our species. Thanks to the Partnership for Public Lands <www.wildontario.org>; NorthWatch <www.web.ca/~nwatch/index.html>; The Georgian Bay Land Trust <www.gblt.org>.

We are very grateful for the support of the following agencies and companies for making the journey possible with the best equipment and supplies and for the assistance necessary to share the journey both en route and after through the Internet and media. **Internet links to all of them can be found on our Web site under Supporters at <www.greatlakesheritagecoast.com>** Thanks to the **Ontario Ministry of Natural Resources Great Lakes Heritage Coast program**, **Tourism Sault Ste. Marie – a division of the Sault Ste. Marie Economic Development Corporation**, **Industry Canada – FedNor**, and **Pictographics**. Special individuals who supported, encouraged, and brought together crucial elements to make the whole project work were Lisa Brygidyr, Peter Burtch, Iain Mettam, Ian McMillan, Tom Dodds, and Louise Paquette. Luke Dalla Bona and Joseph Shulman at Pictographics created and maintained the Web site, while acting as a smoothly running communications headquarters. Austin Comerton of **Mobile Satellite Ventures** provided the satellite phone and unlimited time to communicate stories and photographs. **Smitty's Subspace Communications** provided the invaluable satellite pager and GPS unit. Smitty (Dave) Smith and Luke Dalla Bona kick-started the journey's communications project. Thanks also to Jim Hilsinger and Donna Hilsinger of **Algoma's Water Tower Inn**.

Skipper Izon solved the journey's initial hurdle by building the first McGuffin-Izon Mad River Canoe prototype, a *perfect* Great Lakes canoe. We are most appreciative to all the companies and individuals who helped us put together the equipment system that made our journey a successful, safe, and enjoyable one. Thanks to Skipper, of **Shadow River Boatworks**, Grand Bend, Ontario, for his four-month labour of love; **Confluence Watersports** representing Mad River Canoe, Wilderness Systems, Voyageur, and Wavesport (Buff Grubb, Kelley Woolsey, Tim Brown, and others for whole-hearted support for our journeys and for assistance in developing North American Water Trails); **Duluth Pack** (Bob Entzion); **Cooke Custom Sewing** (Dan Cooke); and **Grey Owl Paddle Company** (Brian Dorfman). Also we gratefully acknowledge Bill Medlin, Steve and Cindy Emerson, John Farchmin, and Chris Gibbs.

Photography is our "voice," and we are indebted to the following for helping us to speak up for wild spaces and wildlife: **Canon Canada**; **DayMen Photo Marketing**, representing Lowepro, Slik, Pelican, SanDisk, Epson, and others (Uwe Mummenhoff and Michael Mayzel); **Fuji Photo Film Canada** (Tim Berry); and **Stan C. Reade Photo**, London, Ontario (Kieran Wallace).

For the healthy food we eat to the comfortable, functional clothes we wear, we thank: **Loblaws Inc.** for President's Choice Organics products (Steve Brown); **Rome's Independent Grocer** (Steve and Kelly Rome); **Blue River Trading Company**, representing SmartWool, Alpine Aire Foods, and Clif Bars (Bud Shirley); **Nutram Pet Products** (Dan Stevenson); **Tilley Endurables** (Alex Tilley); and **Chota Outdoor Gear** (Frank Bryant).

This journey would not have been the wonderful journey it was without the following family, friends, and acquaintances. Thank you all: Jeanette and David Lightwood; Andrew Haill; Jim Coslett and Michele Coslett Goodman; the staff of Sleeping Giant Provincial Park <www.ontarioparks.ca>; Bert Saasto; Gail Jackson; Vivian, Tim, Mirabai, and Fae Alexander; the staff of Rainbow Falls Provincial Park; Ralph, Wendy, Laura, and Christina Roberts; the staff of Neys Provincial Park; Pat and Brian Hicks; the staff of Pukaskwa National Park <www.canadianparks.com>; Ken and Rilla Zak; David Wells; Mary Jo Cullen; Valerie Palmer and Dan Klassen; the staff of Lake Superior Provincial Park; Edna West; Ruth Fletcher and Ward Conway; June and Gerry Demers <www.agawaindiancrafts.com>; June Palmer; Joe and Mary Calleri; Dan and Loretta Sweezey; Gary, Cathie, Brianna, and Colin Meyers; Gayle Russell and Betty Russell; Mayor John Roswell; Carmen Provensano, MP Sault Ste. Marie; Donna Woldanski; Louise Robillard, Sharon Ostberg and the staff of Sault Canal National Historic Site of Canada; Joan Foster; Stuart and Jean Armstrong; the staff of Huron Pines Golf and Country Club; CBC *On the Road Again* crew (Jonathan Craven, Roger Dubois, André Charbonneau, and Wayne Rostad); Stoney Burton; Brent St. Denis, MP Algoma-Manitoulin; Charlie and Jeanne Katz; Maury and Annabelle East and Jennifer East <www.killarney.com>; Maggie Palmer; Randy Daoust and Dallas Daoust; Ted and Tricia Polte; Heather Dale McLaren; Emmaline Madigan; Kenton Otterbein and the staff of Killbear Provincial Park; Katherine Wheatley; and John and Jennifer Wood (Mom and Dad). Thanks to Robin MacIntyre and Enn Poldmaa <www.bellevuevalleylodge.ca>, for delivering food packages, reading the manuscript, and offering valuable suggestions, and for looking after Kalija. Also thanks to CBC Radio hosts Paul Tukker, Gerald Graham, and Dan Lessard for all the enjoyable radio conversations. Thank you once again to everyone at McClelland & Stewart for patience and humour in helping us to consolidate a big story into a comfortable-sized book! With particular thanks to Doug Gibson, Pat Kennedy, Heather Sangster, and Kong Njo.